D0575771

I Like Science!

Exploring the Rain Forest Treetops

with a Scientist

Judith Williams

Enslow Publishers, Inc.

40 Industrial Road   PO Box 38
Box 398   Aldershot
Berkeley Heights, NJ 07922   Hants GU12 6BP
USA   UK
http://www.enslow.com

Contents

Words to Know

canopy (CAN uh pea)—The top area of the rain forest closest to the sky.

epiphyte (EP ih fyt)—A plant that usually grows on another plant or tree. It does not put roots into the tree. It just uses its roots to hold on to branches.

rain forest—A place with lots of trees, plants, and heavy rainfall. The temperature stays warm all year.

harness (HAHR nes)—A set of straps that fits over a climber's legs and waist. A harness is used with ropes to safely climb trees.

light meter (LYT MEE tur)—A tool that measures the amount of light in one place.

What is a rain forest canopy?

The **canopy** is the highest part of the rain forest. From the sky, it looks like a thick roof of treetops, leaves, and plants.

The rain forest canopy is filled
with insects, animals, and plants.
Some of them are found nowhere
else on earth!

4

fruit bat

The living things in the canopy help each other grow—without even trying! A bat eats fruit, then drops the seeds as it flies. Spreading seeds helps more trees grow.

#

Nalini is a forest scientist. She learns how trees live, breathe, and grow in the rain forest.

Scientist Nalini wants to know how the canopy is important to the whole rain forest.

Scientist Nalini studies how canopy plants grow.

Canopies are found in rain forests and cloud forests. Rain forests grow in warm places with lots of rainfall. Cloud forests are a bit different from rain forests.

rain forest

Cloud forests are found in cooler, higher, mountain areas. The canopy trees are smaller and are usually covered with mist, clouds, and rain. Scientist Nalini works in both kinds of canopy forests.

cloud forest

Do animals live in the canopy?

toucan

Yes! Many animals live in the canopy, such as snakes, monkeys, birds, and even earthworms!

Butterflies and other insects make their home here, too. The treetops get more sun and rain than the forest floor does. Many plants, seeds, and fruits grow in the canopy. This means canopy animals have lots to eat.

The Morpho butterfly eats rotting fruit on the forest floor and in the canopy, too.

Plants called epiphytes grow in the canopy. They do not grow in soil like most plants. They grow on tree trunks and branches! Epiphytes use the tall trees of the canopy to get more sunlight and rain.

Epiphytes make their own soil from rotten leaves and roots.

Do scientists go up into the canopy?

Yes. Most canopy animals and plants cannot be studied from the forest floor. Scientists can use a blimp to park a raft on the canopy.

Construction cranes can lift scientists in a basket to reach the canopy. Usually, scientists climb using ropes and **harnesses**. Scientist Nalini is careful not to hurt the trees and the epiphytes when she climbs.

harness

What does scientist Nalini do in the canopy?

She does tests to see what the trees and epiphytes need to grow. She measures branches. Big branches mean the tree is growing well.

What happens in the canopy is important to the whole rain forest.

Scientist Nalini uses light meters.
These tell her how much sunlight
comes through the canopy.

She collects rain in
buckets to measure
how much rain falls.

What other tests does scientist Nalini do?

Scientist Nalini is worried about the earth getting warmer. If this happens, there will be fewer clouds. Then the cloud forest will not be as wet.

Cloud forests and rain forests need lots of water for plants and trees to grow.

Scientist Nalini did an experiment.
She put some epiphytes in a drier
forest nearby. Would they grow with
less cloud water? The epiphytes died.

epiphyte

Lots of dead epiphytes
would show us that the
earth is getting too warm.

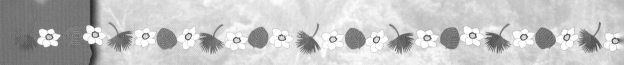

Scientist Nalini invites people to visit the rain forest canopy. Then they can see how the canopy and rain forest need each other to grow well. From high in the canopy, visitors see how important it is to protect the rain forest.

Even rain forests have a dry season when there is less rain. How do some epiphytes hold water to keep growing?

You will need:

- ✔ **one pineapple**
- ✔ **broccoli**
- ✔ **sink**
- ✔ **jar**
- ✔ **water**
- ✔ **measuring cup**

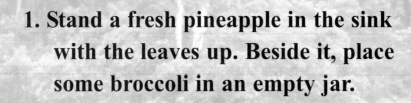

1. Stand a fresh pineapple in the sink with the leaves up. Beside it, place some broccoli in an empty jar.

2. Pour 2 cups of water over each one. Which plant holds water best? The pineapple! It is a relative of some epiphytes.

Some epiphytes hold even more water. These water pockets become home to all kinds of animals, even baby frogs!

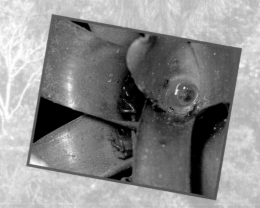

Learn More

Books

Berger, Melvin, and Gilda Berger. *Does It Always Rain in the Rain Forest?* New York: Scholastic Inc., 2002.

Collard, Sneed B. III. *The Forest in the Clouds.* Watertown, Mass.: Charlesbridge Publishing, 2000.

Pirotta, Saviour. *Trees and Plants in the Rain Forest.* Austin, Tex.: Raintree/Steck-Vaughn Company, 1999.

Wilkes, Angela. *Rainforest.* New York: Kingfisher Publications, 2002.

Web Sites

Cloud Forest Alive.
<http://www.cloudforestalive.org/>

Rainforest Education.
<http://www.rainforesteducation.com/>

Index

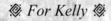 *For Kelly*

Series Literacy Consultant:
Allan A. De Fina, Ph.D.
Past President of the New Jersey Reading Association
Professor, Department of Literacy Education
New Jersey City University

Science Consultant:
Nalini Nadkarni, Ph.D.
Professor of Environmental Studies
The Evergreen State College
President, International Canopy Network

Note to Teachers and Parents: The **I Like Science!** series supports the National Science Education Standards for K–4 science, including content standards "Science as a human endeavor" and "Science as inquiry." The Words to Know section introduces subject-specific vocabulary, including pronunciation and definitions. Early readers may require help with these new words.

Library of Congress Cataloging-in-Publication Data

Williams, Judith (Judith A.)
    Exploring the rain forest treetops with a scientist / Judith Williams.
        p. cm. — (I like science!)
    Includes bibliographical references (p.   ).
    ISBN 0-7660-2294-3 (hardcover)
    1. Rain forests—Juvenile literature. [1. Rain forests. 2. Scientists. 3. Occupations.] I. Title. II. Series.
QH86.W556 2004
578.734-dc22

2003026958

Printed in the United States of America

10 9 8 7 6 5 4 3 2 1

Photo Credits: © Corel Corporation, pp. 21, 22 (top) ; © 2004 Gary Braasch, pp. 3, 6, 8, 9, 11, 12, 13; The International Canopy Network (ICAN), 5, 14, 16, 17, 18, 19, 20; © Ken Lucas/Visuals Unlimited, p. 7; © Reto Siegenthaler, p. 22 (bottom); © Tom Ulrich/Visuals Unlimited, p. 10; Therese Frare/ICAN, pp. 4, 15.

Cover Photo: Therese Frare/ICAN